197

DAN
MARINO

*(Photo on
front cover.)*

**Dan Marino
runs with the
ball after failing
to find an open
receiver.**

*(Photo on
previous pages.)*

**Coach Don
Shula talks with
quarterback
Dan Marino.**

Photography supplied by Wide World Photos Inc.

Library of Congress Cataloging-in-Publication Data
Rambeck, Richard.
Dan Marino / Richard Rambeck.
p. cm.
Summary: Surveys the football career of the Miami Dolphins'
record-breaking quarterback, Dan Marino.
ISBN 1-56766-313-3 ((lib. bdg.)

1. Marino, Dan, 1961-   --Juvenile literature. 2. Football
players --United States --Biography --Juvenile literature.
3. Miami Dolphins (Football team) --Juvenile liturature.
[1. Marino, Dan, 1961-   . 2. Football players.]
I. Title
GV939.M29R36   1996   96-7670
796.332'092 — dc20   CIP
[B]   AC

DAN
MARINO

BY RICHARD RAMBECK

The quarterback drops back to pass. As he moves backward, he looks down the field for someone to throw to. Suddenly, a receiver has a step on his defender. The quarterback sees this instantly and throws the ball, hitting the receiver in the hands for a first down. No quarterback in the history of the National Football League has done this better than Dan Marino of the Miami Dolphins. If a receiver is open, Marino will see him and deliver the ball on target almost every time.

During the 1995 season, Marino wrote his name in the NFL record book again and again. He broke Fran Tarkenton's career records for most pass

Tarkenton's career records for most pass attempts and completions, touchdown passes, and yards gained. When Marino broke Tarkenton's mark for most completions in NFL history, the former quarterback sent Marino a message that appeared on the scoreboard at Miami's Joe Robbie Stadium during the game. Tarkenton's message said what almost everybody in the NFL thought about Marino.

"You are one of the greatest quarterbacks who has ever played," Tarkenton wrote. "You've earned it. You deserve it. I'm honored that you're the one who's breaking [the record]." Marino set a lot of records and had another solid year in 1995, but the Dolphins' season ended

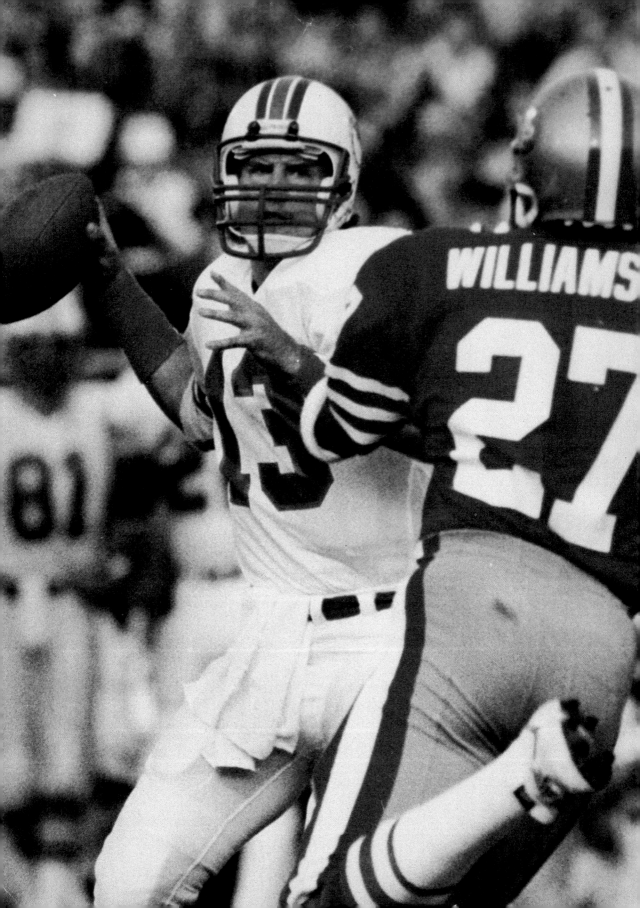

in the first round of the American Football Conference playoffs. Miami lost to Buffalo 37-22. Many experts had picked the Dolphins to win the AFC title and go to the Super Bowl. Instead, Miami finished 9-7.

"I'm like everyone else," Marino said after losing to the Bills. "I felt coming into this year we would be in the Super Bowl. It didn't work out. I've done a lot of things in my career, but I've never won a Super Bowl." After the season, Miami coach Don Shula, who had won more games than any NFL coach in history, retired. The Dolphins then hired former Dallas Cowboys coach Jimmy Johnson. Unlike Marino, Johnson had won the Super Bowl—twice, in fact, as coach of the Cowboys.

"The only thing he wants is to win games and the Super Bowl," Marino said of his new coach. "That's why he has taken the job. And that's all I want to do—win games and have a chance to win the championship. That's what makes me happy." Dan Marino was one of the reasons Johnson agreed to coach the Dolphins. Johnson knew Marino was the type of player around whom he could build a Super Bowl team. But Johnson also knew he needed more than just Marino to win a championship.

"I think Dan Marino is a great player," Johnson said. "When you have a player as good as Dan Marino, you sometimes fall into a trap of letting him try to win the

game for you all the time." When he came into the NFL in 1983, Marino did seem like a player who could win games by himself. In his first few years in the league, Marino was almost unstoppable. In his rookie year, he threw 20 touchdown passes and only six interceptions, leading the Dolphins to the AFC Eastern Division title.

Miami, however, lost to Seattle in the playoffs, falling two games short of reaching the Super Bowl. The following season, Marino had the greatest year an NFL quarterback has ever had, even to this day. He threw for 5,084 yards, a record that still stands. He tossed 48 touchdown passes, another record that still stands—and that some experts

15

believe will never be broken. The Dolphins finished 14-2, won the AFC East title, and then made it to the Super Bowl.

In the Super Bowl, Marino's Dolphins faced Joe Montana and the San Francisco 49ers, a match-up of two of the best quarterbacks in history. Marino got off to an excellent start, completing nine of his first 10 passes. At the end of the first quarter, the Dolphins had a 10-7 lead. The second period, however, was a nightmare for Miami. The 49ers scored three touchdowns to take a 28-10 lead. The Dolphins wound up losing 38-16. Despite the defeat, Marino and his teammates believed they would soon make it back to the Super Bowl.

The Dolphins won another division title in 1985, but lost to the New England Patriots in the AFC championship game. Marino had another great season in 1986, throwing for 4,746 yards and 44 touchdowns. Miami, however, didn't even make the playoffs. In fact, the Dolphins didn't reach the playoffs again until 1990. Marino, though, still had outstanding seasons. Former Pittsburgh Steelers quarterback Terry Bradshaw, who was Marino's idol, said the Miami star was an "exceptional quarterback."

"Throwing for that many yards is mind-boggling," Bradshaw said of Marino, "especially when you consider that since his rookie year he has been a marked man. Teams were saying, 'We have to stop [Miami's] passing attack.' They've done everything in the world to stop it. And they can't, and they won't, and they never will." Vinny Testaverde, who played college football at the University of Miami, said Marino is like the Michael Jordan of the NFL. Marino, Testaverde said, can do things no one else can do.

"You look at his accomplishments and how quickly he's done those things, and you have to be amazed by them," said Testaverde, who has played quarterback for Tampa Bay and Cleveland in the NFL. Marino, however, didn't accomplish much of anything in 1993. He tore his Achilles tendon early in the season and was out for the rest of the year. Some Miami fans

wondered if he would ever be able to play again. Tearing an Achilles tendon is a serious injury that forces many athletes to retire.

When the 1994 season began, Marino was ready to play. He led the Dolphins to an AFC Eastern Division championship. Miami then beat Kansas City in the first round of the playoffs before losing a heartbreaker to the San Diego Chargers, 22-21. Again, Marino lost out on a chance to make it to the NFL title game. "I don't want to walk away from the game without getting to another Super Bowl," he said. "But I love playing and I can feel good about my career." Yes, he can, because he might be the best quarterback ever.